I0008457

CONTENTS

Don't Panic.

- Douglas Adams, The Hitchhiker's Guide to the Galaxy

INTRODUCTION

There are many reasons I included the quote from Douglas Adams on the previous page. They are the words that are enshrined on the cover of the Hitchhiker's Guide to the Galaxy (HG2G) as it is carted around the galaxy by unknown numbers of beings in Adams' epic trilogy. The creators of the Hitchhiker's Guide had put it there for one reason: to keep readers from panicking over the strange circumstances they may encounter or the complexity of the guide itself.

In that same respect, I think it is an incredibly accurate sentiment to remember when trying to change careers. If you are reading this book, then that is precisely what you are doing. If not, this book may not be for you and I can advise any number of other volumes.

This book is short by design. It is a meta-educational tool. It is a guidebook to help you learn how to become a software developer and guide you in the process. You will find lessons in here about some general computer science theory to give you introductions. I'll provide you some general ideas of toolsets and resources. What I won't do in this book is teach you a specific language.

Don't Panic. I don't need to teach you a specific language in this book. You can easily learn a language by any thousands of tutorials online or with manuals, coding games, hacker challenges, etc. I'll introduce you to some languages, what they should do, and where you can find potential careers. But I will not try to teach you Java or Visual Basic .NET. For one, I haven't used .NET much, but that's ok. Honestly, once you learn one language, picking up another isn't horrible. It will take time, but the learning curve isn't as steep for each new language you learn.

At this point, you may ask, "What the hell?"

There's a secret I discovered during sixteen years in software development, across a half dozen roles and getting a Bachelor's Degree in Computer Science. The secret is that you don't need a degree to get into this career. You can get into development with a high school equivalency and a very tenacious attitude. You might find an easier time with getting a job with some sort of college degree, but I've known people that didn't complete or even go to college and worked in dev and engineering. I've met and helped train people moving from mostly non-technical roles into development. I've met people that did it on their own.

If you still don't believe me, then just remember a few things. How did people get into coding and computer science before there were computer science degrees offered by colleges? While most people that don't go to college won't become billionaires, there are examples of exactly that happening. Bill Gates and Steve Jobs both dropped out of college, so did Michael Dell. Twitter CEO Jack Dorsey, Mark Zuckerburg and Elon Musk all dropped out too. I'm not expecting this book will be the impetus for any billion-dollar careers, if it is, please remember to leave me reviews and possibly a trust fund. However, I would expect anyone willing to follow the advice in this book to be able to start a career.

That's who this guide is meant for, the people that want to get into coding and not spend $10,000 - $100,000 to do it. I'll take you through how to learn certain things, what to learn, some very basic Computer Science (CS) concepts, and a guide to picking languages to learn. Later in this book, we'll discuss what to look for during your job search, what to expect when you're on the job and how to work towards continuing success.

Yes, that sounds like a lot. No, this book is not that thick or big. Don't Panic. This book will not be your only resource, it's just your guide to tell you where else you need to find your learning tools. All you will need is a computer of some sort (I'm not picky), this book (look at you, all prepared), and a lot of tenacity.

CHAPTER 1

How to Learn

"Human beings, who are almost unique in having the ability to learn from the experience of others, are also remarkable for their apparent disinclination to do so."

— *Douglas Adams*

The problem I have with a lot of legislated public school curriculum from when I was young was that it didn't teach you how to learn. They like to drill in a lot of memorization, so you can take a standardized test, pass it, and some legislators can get a bonus. That doesn't really teach you a good way to find new information.

The goal of this chapter is to give you resources to help you find these new things to learn. While learning to code, and especially in the workplace, you will never know everything. Having these resources and knowing good ways to use and interact with them will help you to find the answers quicker and get back to the process.

Logic and Reasoning

When you boil it down, all coding and building computer applications come down to logic and reason. Given an input of X, we interpret or transform to Y. To know what to build, you have to utilize both deductive and inductive reasoning to construct the logic around algorithms and programs. This is true of building programs from scratch, working with an existing code base to add new features, and troubleshooting/fixing bugs in deployed systems.

Inductive Reasoning is a process of drawing a conclusion based on some supply of observable evidence. Good examples of this would include estimating user adoption based on a previous model. Let's say you're rebuilding a site for a new server. You know your average user load is 300 user sessions per hour. This can help you gauge how much memory, processors and bandwidth you'll need as a minimum to meet the site's requirements. As another example, suppose you have a piece of code throwing an error. You are given error stack traces that tell you the lines of code ran up to the error being encountered. You are also given a dump of the application structure and the user's session that caused the error. Based on those pieces of evidence, you can use that to determine what is causing the error and fix that bug.

Deductive Reasoning is the process of reaching a logical conclusion by building on one or more premises. This kind of logic is utilized heavily in coding, especially when planning out a new application or new features. Such as a login feature. We could say

- Our Users generally all have a Facebook login
- We don't want to maintain user login on our own
- Therefore we will integrate FB Single Sign On for Authentication

I don't want to dwell long on these subjects, but both are definitely useful throughout an entire software development career. As you start on tutorials, projects, getting into jobs, etc., you'll use both daily too.

How to Google

Search engines will be a necessary aspect of your life as a coder. Given the extensive nature of languages and computers overall, no employer will expect you to be so expert on everything that you can store the whole of that knowledge base in your memory. Knowing extra tricks for how to use a search engine like Google though, can help you spend less time digging through results. Here are very simple ways to refine your search strategies.

"Quotation Marks" Wrapping your search phrase in quotation marks will let you search for results containing that exact phrase. This is extremely useful when searching for the meaning of a specific error. For example, searching for null pointer exception may bring back a lot of explanations for a lot of different languages. But using "null pointer exception java" will require the whole of those statements to be matched in the query and your results will be directly related to how to fix or prevent a null pointer in Java specifically.

- Dash Putting a dash before a word in your search phrase will exclude that word from your search results. This may not seem useful until you find there are a lot of open-source software projects that use names from something famous. For example, Apache has projects like Kafka. Kafka manages services but was also named for Bohemian novelist Franz Kafka. So, if you are more interested in the software project, you might google the phrase Apache Kafka -franz. A similar example would be Capistrano. Capistrano being a software package named after a city that swallows fly back to annually. So, searching for Capistrano -swallows may give more information on the deployment tool rather than results about birds returning to San Juan Capistrano.

~ Tilde That strange little character on your keyboard to the left of the 1 and just above the tab key.

Using a tilde will allow you to tell Google to include synonyms in a search phrase. An example of this would be searching Java ~exception handling, which would cover errors and other types of issues if you want to know how to deal with errors and exceptions.

Site: Using the site specifier will make Google search only that site. This could be useful if you know something is on a certain site, but don't want to spend time browsing and searching the whole site. For example, Apache default port site:apache.org would help me quickly find what the default port number an Apache server would run. Apache is a very popular web server, and knowing what port it runs on by default is a typical thing a developer would need to know.

| Vertical Bar A single vertical bar between words acts as an OR operator for Google. An example would be if you want to look at professions that deal with certain languages or technology, you could Google: Java | JavaScript | SQL | Node

.. Two Periods This will allow your search to include a span between numbers. For example, Entry Level Developer $45000..$50000 would help you find where to find a job as an entry-level developer with a salary between $45,000 and $50,000

There are many other tricks and specialized search utilities in Google. These few and just learning to hone what consists of a good Google search phrase vs. a bad one is honestly half of the career of a developer. A lot of non-technical people see developers and think of this fictional "Hackerman". They believe hackerman has all of the secrets for computer programming, hacking, networking, etc. just up in their head and that hackerman sits down knowing literally everything they will do before they do it.

That is as much an urban legend as Bloody Mary. I don't know a single developer in any language or job title that can fulfill this hackerman ideal. I'm likely to Google 10 times a day minimum, because some things just aren't known and some things just slide from memory. I may encounter something I've never worked on before, so I'll search about it. I may even just be working on something I have done before, but it's been a while since I've created a specific kind of index on a database table. So, I'll Google the syntax around creating the index.

Documentation

One of the oldest comments in online forums to, "How do I do x" is "RTFM". This very simple acronym stands for Read The F*#@ing Manual. Yes, people in tech curse and use "foul language". A lot. I'll try to avoid it as much as possible in this manual, mainly to get a lower rating and higher sales on Amazon, but not to save your innocence. We'll cover this more in later chapters, but the lesson is:

the best place to start is with the actual manual written by the people that created something. For example, if you want to learn the Angular framework, going to angular.io and reading the documentation put together by Google and the Angular team is a logical first step.

Not all systems/languages are created equally though. Sometimes the documentation and manuals just suck. In those cases, Googling examples and tutorials may be more helpful and explanatory than RTFM.

Tutorials

A lot of developers and members on projects want to make sure their tech gets used. Rather than making you read something that may be as hard to understand as a stereo manual from 1985 or the Handbook for the Recently Deceased, they'll publish easier to follow tutorials. These will generally assume you have prior knowledge but will list the previous requirements and the general audience. These can be as simple as building your first Hello World project in Java, How To set up a development environment for JavaScript coding in Visual Studio Code, or as complex as Dealing with multi-subscriber queues in Rabbit MQ. Google and search engines can help you find many of them, usually specific to your own use cases.

GitHub

GitHub is an online code repository. Origin story time. A long time ago, when there were fewer developers, it generally wasn't an issue for multiple people to be working on something at the same time. As more people came into programming jobs, program complexity grew, and the amount of code for projects expanded, a problem was created. The problem was how can more than one person work on a single file of code without causing issues with everyone working on it? The solution became code repositories. A code repository at it's most basic level is a storage system that will track changes in code as people make them. There have been multiple programs to help solve this, popular code repositories included CVS (Continuious Versioning System), Subversion (SVN), and Mercurial (HG).

At the time of this printing, one of the most popular code repository systems is called Git. Git comes with many features that other code repos have made popular, but also offers a central online place to signup called GitHub. GitHub allows you to host your repositories, expose open source projects to the world, and collaborate with a large community of developers. Learning how Git works and how to navigate GitHub will be crucial to your journey to finding a job in coding. For a homework assignment for this chapter, run through some tutorials for Git.

Sign up for an account, download Git, follow examples on creating your first repository, and learning about how to do things like commits, branching, and pull requests.

Aside from being a great place for you and the teams you will be working on to host your projects, GitHub is a valuable research and learning tool. You can search GitHub for keywords and filter results on language to find open repositories and projects. Using that, you can use GitHub to help you learn from real-life examples of how a project is started, built and brought to a production-ready system.

Stack Overflow

Usually when you search for something tech-related, the top results will likely be from Stack Overflow. Stack Overflow is an online community for tech questions. They have expanded in the last half-decade to help specializations, but overall you can find many questions answered on Stack Overflow (SO). In recent years, they've listed job postings too. SO is a fantastic resource for helping to find information, understand how things work, and even getting career advice.

At times, you may find the problem you are facing is a newer issue or unique enough that no one else has asked about it before. Asking about it on SO can be an excellent option. It may take a while to still solve your problem, but the community on SO is very responsive. Before you ask that question though, read through the following section.

Online Community Interaction

Online communities are great places for meeting new friends, networking, and getting answers to questions. However, they can also be judgemental and havens to the worst trolls known to humanity. Here are tips for interacting in a place like SO without becoming an online pariah.

Research Never just automatically jump onto a forum or SO and just ask a question without some research first. Many users will find this incredibly annoying since it dilutes the forum with potentially duplicate issues. Try different ways to find similar problems to yours that have already been asked. If you find a topic/thread that is similar but doesn't give an answer that works for you or is slightly different, try commenting on that existing thread. By commenting, you are getting the attention of people that already had dealt with the same issue and may know how to fix the problem for you. It also shows that you're paying attention to the community and not just throwing duplicate questions out. Another option may be to send a direct message to the Original Poster (OP) or to one of the users that answered the question.

Be Nice It takes less effort than you think, and avoiding sarcasm and mean comments will get you very far with other users. Remember, you are here to learn, but also after some time, you may be teaching by answering other people's questions. Don't treat other users like Snape treats anyone but a Slytherin. Remember, every user on that community is in the same boat.

Upvote/Downvote If you see something that can help you or you find a topic useful, be sure to upvote it. Upvoting will help it receive more attention and doesn't cost you a dime. Downvote topics you think are detrimental to the community, like something that may not belong on that forum or promote some sort of wrong/dishonest information.

Self-promotion Don't do this. Keep that to LinkedIn and Facebook. Never start a thread on SO about how you are a beginner coder looking for work as an entry-level dev in any language. It will all only end in tears. The forum is not there for people to find you a job, and many users will tell you the same thing in very nasty comments. The same goes for if you have a service and you're trying to advertise. SO and coding forums are meant to help people find solutions to their problems, not for you to sell your goods and services. Keep your advertising separate. It could even get you banned from there altogether.

Assignment: Join and Tutorials

Take what you've learned from this chapter and apply it for about an hour. Set up accounts at places like GitHub and Stack Overflow. Run through the tutorials and documentation on Git. See if you can be able to utilize the tutorials on GitHub and your new-found Googling skills to answer:

-        What's a branch
-        What is a commit and what should be included in a commit message
-        How do you merge a new commit from another user into your local repo?

Also, take time on SO to set up an account and read some issues. You may not know the answers, and that's fine. Sometimes, just reading some problems and seeing how others approach debugging/discussing them will help you learn the process. This kind of entry-level wallflower interaction will help you gain a better understanding of how to interact on SO yourself.

CHAPTER 2

What to Learn

"What I mean is that if you really want to understand something, the best way is to try and explain it to someone else. That forces you to sort it out in your own mind. And the more slow and dim-witted your pupil, the more you have to break things down into more and more simple ideas. And that's really the essence of programming. By the time you've sorted out a complicated idea into little steps that even a stupid machine can deal with, you've certainly learned something about it yourself."

— *Douglas Adams,* **Dirk Gently's Holistic Detective Agency**

T he world of software is big. There's a lot out there. When you get into the job titles and what you want to do, there are a lot of choices. You have front end development, back end development, full stack, dev-ops, database administration, etc. Even within each of those titles, you get granular specialization. If you want to work in front end dev, do you specialize in only pure JavaScript? Do you lean on a certain framework like React or Angular. For backend, do you microservice with node, or do you work in Ruby, or do you build up a larger scale .NET or Java server? If you use Java, do you run WebSphere, Tomcat or any other number of container-based runtime engines? There's a lot to learn and a lot to unpack. Don't panic and just ignore some things for now if they don't make sense.

Hitchhiker's Guide to CS

One thing any employer will be looking for is a basic understanding of some computer science concepts. Don't Panic. This will not be a dive into the rabbit hole, just a very brief skimming. Some examples will be given in Pseudocode. **Pseudocode** is code that mimics actual code, but may not apply to any specific language. In jobs or interviews, you will use Pseudocode to mock a problem and work through how something should work. It's really to get a gist, and actually be implemented later.

Object Oriented Programming (OOP)

Many employers will expect you to understand Object Oriented Programming (OOP) as a core concept to software development. This sounds scary, but don't panic. It means that you build the program in blocks of objects. An object is just a way of expressing a part of your program as a group of properties and methods. Properties are bits of data your object stores and methods are things it can do to that data.

To conceptualize this, think of a car. If you described a car, how would you describe it? Things like type (sedan, coupe, hatchback, sports, etc.), color, passenger count would be properties. Other aspects of the car, like accelerate, brake, and other functions the car does would be the methods. So, properties are things that describe the car and methods are things it can do.

In OOP, there are four main concepts: Abstraction, Polymorphism, Interitance, and Encapsulation.

Variables/Properties

In the code you write, you will have the necessity to store data. In an object, these bits of data are called variables or properties. All languages will have documentation regarding how to define these and what is valid. Depending on the language, variables may require a type, these are called strongly typed languages, like Java. Some languages, like JavaScript, have a looser typing. For example, in our earlier concept of a car we would have a property for color. In Java, a default red color would be defined   as:

```
1 private String color = "red";
```

In JavaScript, a typeless language, we can define it simply   as:

```
1 var color = "red";
```

The differences between the two being that the Java example specified a scope (private) and a type (String). Strong typing can help better enforce business logic, though it can cause issues if used improperly.

Basic Logical Operators

In most programming languages, you will encounter logic operators. These will create the computational representation of the business rules. They guide the program to do something if conditions are met. Here are some of the most basic ones you'll encounter.

== A double equals sign in most languages will be a test for equality. It says does the left side equal the right.

!= An exclamation sign is typically the symbol to mean not. So, en exclamation and equals is the way of saying the left side does not equal the right.

&&, || In most coding languages, double amper-sands will be a logical way to say AND, double pipes means OR. (The Pipe character on the slash key be-tween enter and delete on most keyboards) Used with logical statements to test for true and false, you can check multiple conditions at once. Such as (This AND That) or (This == 5 && That == 6), which will mean this has to equal 5 and that has to equal 6 for something to happen. Similarly, if it were an OR, then either this equal 5 or that equal 6 for the execution to occur.

<,>,>=, <= Comparitors to ask less than, greater than, greater than or equal to, and less than or equal to.

+,-,/,* Mathematical operators, for addition, sub-traction, division and multiplication

% In most languages, the operator for mathemat-ical modulus or modulo. Basically, remainder after division. Can be read as 8 % 5 = 3, as in 8 / 5 = 1 re-mainder 3, but we only get the 3 with modulus.

++, - - In most languages, these are increment and decrement operators, so if you have a variable i that is an integer currently equal to 9, i++ will become 10, i— will be 8.

If/ElseIf/Else: If statements are just like they sound. If a condition is met, then something exe-cutes. Else, if another condition is met, then a different piece executes. Else, if nothing matches, then something else can execute. As an example, let's say from our Car concept that the price of the car changes based on certain colors, we could write that as:

```
1   if(color == "red") {
2       price = 10000;
3   } else if(color == "black" || color == "blue") {
4       price = 12000;
5   else {
6       price = 9500;
7   }
```

Switch Statement A switch statement is like an extensive if statement made compact. It tests a single condition and executes code based on which condition matches. Using the same example in the If/Else above, we can just write:

```
1   switch (color) {
2       case "red":
3           price = 10000;
4           break;
5       case "black", "blue":
6           price = 12000;
7           break;
8       default:
9           price = 9500;
10          break;
11  }
```

Looping

Loops are useful programming blocks. They allow you to execute something either a set number of times or until some condition changes. There are three basic types of loops in most programming languages: **For, While,** and **Do While**,

For: A For loop will execute some piece of code during a set number of iterations. Usually, this requires a start point, an end point, and an incrementer. Let's say we want to print to a screen Hello 500 times. We could do something like this:

```
1    for (int i = 1; i <= 500; i++) {
2        Print "Hello";
3    }
```

In the example, we declared an integer i as 1 as our start, that the code would execute as long as i is less than or equal to 500, and increment i by 1 each step.

While: A while loop will start with a condition and execute the code as long as the condition is still true. It will differ from a Do While by the fact that it checks the condition before execution, which could mean that the condition is never met and the code won't execute at all. A similar example is below.

```
1    int i = 1;
2    while(i <= 500) {
3        print "Hello";
4        i++;
5    }
```

Do ... While: A Do While loop is exactly the same as the While loop, but it doesn't check the condition until after the code executes. Our same example would be:

```
1    int i = 1;
2    do {
3        print "Hello";
4        i++;
5    } while(i <= 500)
```

The only fundamental difference between the two is when the condition is checked. This could be useful based on your business requirements.

Algorithms

An algorithm is a basic set of rules to be followed for calculations or problem-solving. An example of an algorithm could be as simple as sorting the alphabet from A to Z when it's out of order. It can be something more complex as well, such as the sequence of operations for diagnostics and checks prior to an aircraft alerting a pilot he is safe to fly.

As you get towards more complex algorithms, you will likely find that it's too much to look at just one algorithm for a problem, but you would need to address multiple algorithms. For example, with the aircraft, the overall requirement is pre-flight safety checks and diagnostics. That list could be quite long as there are a lot of parts, sensors, etc., in an aircraft. The algorithm would, therefore, call smaller routines or other algorithms in the process, such as a single algorithm for checking adequate fuel supply.

Input/Output

Generally, a program or algorithm comes down to data making changes or being viewed. If there's no purpose to what's being executed, then there's no point to executing anything at all. That means the program requires some data to go in, a transformation of some sort occurs, then data comes back out.

Take something like Facebook, for example. When you ask to log into Facebook, you provide user credentials as input and an algorithm determines if you are allowed access (output). When you've logged in, Facebook takes your user information as input, looks up your friends, the posts they think you want to see, etc., and displays all that to you as output on your screen.

Inputs and outputs can vary widely from variables passed into a function, a database connection made from an application, or even sensors connected to a machine to measure the temperature of the air.

Big O Notation

Big O Notation is a mathematical Notation used to describe complexity or programmatic impact. It helps to describe what impact algorithms can have on an overall application based on worst-case scenarios. For example, a program with a piece that is supposed to sort a standard deck of 52 playing cards.

If the deck were stored in a way it was already sorted, then the sort would have a Big O Notation of $O(1)$ meaning, it only would execute one time.

If we had an out of order deck, but the ability to sort it by looping it just one time (once for each of 52 cards), then our Big O score would be $O(n)$, as n equals the length of the deck.

If the deck is out of order, and we used a worse algorithm to sort, then our complexity increases to $O(n^2)$. Which means the code is executed n squared times $(52 * 52 = 2704)$ to sort the deck at a worst-case scenario.

If we find a better sorting algorithm, we may find our executions at worst case for an out of order deck close to a notation of $O(\log n)$. This is higher than $O(1)$, but will run better than $O(n)$. It's the logarithm (inverse square) of n. In the deck of cards example, $\log 52 = 1.72$.

The reason for knowing this is to determine how complex you can or want your algorithms. Writing something $O(n^2)$ may be very simple and take little developer time to implement and test. Writing it to meet $O(\log n)$ may require a lot more time to ensure the algorithm matches that expectation. The requirement may be mitigated, too, if your expected data set is small or large. In a server with massive amounts of memory, sorting at $O(n^2)$ for a dataset of 10 elements is nothing at all. But trying to do a sort of 10,000 elements at $O(n^2)$ on an older Windows machine from 1999 may be noticeable and worth the time to find a way to reach $O(n)$ or $O(\log n)$.

Interviewers may expect you to answer a question on this, and you may use it on the job day to day. It varies role to role and company to company. It sounds complicated, but Don't Panic.

Recursion

Another topic you may be asked about in interviews is recursion. It is the idea of writing something that can call itself to continually execute. A good example of how this can be useful would be in tree traversal. A tree is a kind of data structure that one object will have 0 - n child objects of the same type. A tree can be useful for storing items in order or in a hierarchy, but sometimes traversal can be tricky. Traversing it with loops can be problematic, but using recursion, you can write a search function that will check the current object, then call the same search function on each of the child objects. In turn, that function call on the child objects will call the search function on the children of those children, and so on until either the item is found or no children exist.

Something to beware of in recursion is to write to be sure it can hit an end and return back or exit.

Otherwise, you can create what is known as an infinite loop. This is a situation where your program is now stuck in the same code segment and will run until you either kill it or it kills itself via exhausting all memory.

Compiled vs Interpreted

Different languages run in different ways. Some languages are compiled. That means you write the code, then you run it through a compiler. The compiler will do some checking and translate the code down into a more basic set of instructions for a targeted runtime or type of computer to be able to execute. An example of this would be Java. Code is written in Java, then a Java Development Kit (JDK) can compile it down to byte code that is executed via a Java Runtime Environment (JRE).

Interpreted languages don't use a compiler. The program is written and then executed through some runtime or standard program. Examples of this are HTML or JavaScript. In these cases, you write the code, then it is executed through the browser, which will interpret the language into what you use on a web page or web application.

Machine Learning

Machine learning is a specialized area of programming. It can also encompass data analytics. Basically, it's the concept of making an adaptive program that can take input and learn from it to adjust the program's own output. Take a self-driving car, for example. If programmed with just the actual driving rules, it could decide that the old lady jay-walking across the street doesn't legally exist and run her down. Or it could believe that people will always stop at red lights. By learning that not all people will stop for a red, could save your life when a plumber in a work van late for a job runs the light going 50 mph.

Software Development Life Cycle

The Software Development Life Cycle (SDLC) is simply the process used for building a piece of software. This could be something as large as an enterprise-level application with millions of users, or a small add-on to an internal application. At the simplest level, it is a cycle of Planning, Analysis, Design, Implementation and Maintenance, often leading back into planning again. There are variations to this, but it can be another point you should learn and familiarize yourself with before getting to a stage with interviews. In relation to the SDLC, there are also variations on how to approach a project. The two primary leaders for processes to manage a project with software engineering have been either Waterfall or Agile.

Waterfall

Waterfall is an approach at managing a project that focuses on longer stages that are never revisited. If you looked at the five stages of the SDLC mentioned previously with this approach, you would view an entire project being addressed over a long period with each of the stages as its own waterfall spilling down. If the estimate is that the project may take six months, then you may spend three weeks or more in planning, then a few more weeks in analysis, a couple of weeks in design, three months in implementation and a month or more in maintenance. Strict followers of this methodology will tell you that once one part of the SDLC is done, it is not revisited. That can cause problems though. For example, how do you address sudden changes or encountering an unknown? Project managers will tell you that if you plan well enough, there should be no unknowns and sudden changes will just have to wait for the next cycle. Basically that what is agreed upon in planning is the entirety of what will be implemented. Also, project managers don't find it funny when you tell them you have a salmon trying to go back upstream to spawn.

Agile

Agile is a different approach to the same problem. It focuses on the SDLC in a different manner, though. With agile, you break up your work into set length Sprints of work. For example, at a lot of companies I've been on staff use a two-week Sprint cycle because one week is too short and four weeks is too long. There is a development team involved that consists of developers, designers and usually testers. A Scrum Master facilitates the agile process and tries to keep meetings on task. Finally, there's a Product Owner, who is the source of the business knowledge and requirements for the software being developed.

The goal is that the development team together with a Product Owner and a Scrum Master can agree on an amount of work to be completed in a Sprint. At the end of the Sprint, what they have done should be a demonstrable and releasable piece or addition to a piece of software. The releasable aspect may not be as focused sometimes, or different teams may agree to a release cadence (frequency) that is varied from the Sprint cycle. Perhaps they agree to have a release cycle of every two or four sprints.

A lot of free resources are online for learning more about the Agile process and methodology. Many people even take on training and make a successful career of being an Agile Coach or Scrum Master and will never write a single line of code. A great place to start is by reading the Agile Manifesto. Practice your new-found Googling skills to find the Agile Manifesto.

Programming Languages

In HG2G, Douglas Adams solved all language

issues for the varying alien species across the galaxy with a creature called a Babel Fish. You slip the little leech-like fish in your ear and it feeds on brain waves while also translating all incoming speech into something your brain can understand.

Sadly, developers don't have something so simple. We have a multitude of languages. I will not be able to teach them all in this book. As a person eager to get straight into a job, you don't want to learn them all either.

I know you're asking, "But Joel, how will I know which one to learn?"

That's something that should become clearer to you as you move forward and with a research assignment to help you pick what is right for you.

Assignment: Language Research

For this assignment, you'll need to make a minor decision. Decide what kind of development role interests you. General web developers will basically put together layouts and user interfaces. A Front End Developer is similar but will require a deeper understanding of JavaScript, TypeScript, and/or Single Page Application (SPA) Frameworks like React, Vue, or Angular. Back End Developers will deal with more server-level logic and handle connectivity between clients and data sources while enforcing some business rules. Full Stack Developers will need to know all of the above.

DevOps engineers are more situated in between

an IT department (handles all the servers with the blinky lights) and Developers. They handle things like scans for code issues, security concerns, and Continous Integration/Continuous Delivery (CI/CD).

A Database engineer will deal primarily with just systems that store data. That could be a simple old fashioned Structured Query Language (SQL) based database, or a clustered MongoDB system, etc. They typically require certifications and a lot of experience, but an entry-level DBA can still expect to make a decent living and work towards those certifications with their employer.

Think about what kind of development may interest you. If you are visually oriented, look at web development or front end. If you enjoy a lot more math and computational challenges, then you could look into back end or dev ops.

Now look at sites like LinkedIn or Glassdoor and see what are the job opportunities. You'll want to be clear on where you want to be as well. If you want to stay in Herndon, VA, then use that for your basis in the jobs search. If your goal is to work for a company like Amazon and move to Seattle, then search for that location. This will help you to know what languages are expected to be known for those various roles. An entry-level software engineer in New York may be expected to know Java, while one in Chicago may be expected to know Visual Studio .NET.

Take at least a few hours to research this carefully and make a decision of 2-3 languages to read more about and doing some simple Hello World style tutorials. That will help you decide which you will be happier with and more comfortable understanding. Search specifically for entry-level jobs when looking at these career sites. Most will help you get an idea of salary expectations too.

CHAPTER 3

Level 0

"A learning experience is one of those things that says, 'You know that thing you just did? Don't do that."

— *Douglas Adams,* **The Salmon of Doubt**

You can learn a lot from tutorials, manuals, YouTube videos and more. However, you can't put a listing of tutorials and manuals on a resume or your LinkedIn account. No hiring manager will be impressed by the number of manuals you've read. Hiring managers will be impressed by actual experience. Herein comes our chicken and egg problem. You generally can't get an entry-level job without some experience, and you can't get any experience without a job. This chapter will discuss how to do that and solve your chicken and egg problem.

Don't just skip straight into this step, though. I really do believe the audience that gains the most from this book are people that can give themselves part-time to changing their careers. There is value in taking three hours a day, four to five times a week to just spend learning before you jump into the rest of this book.

Coding Bootcamps

In the last few years, a number of institutions and firms have sprung up around the United States that offer coding boot camps. Like the military boot camps they are named after, a coding boot camp will be an immersive class to teach you job skills, project management and teamwork. They run anywhere between eight weeks and six months, with costs varying. The average tuition costs are about $12,000 at the time of writing. Tuition can range though, anywhere between a few thousand dollars and up.

You might decide that a boot camp would be the best route for yourself. For some, it is. If you don't have to support yourself or a family and can apply yourself full time to a two to six-month program then it can be a great fit. However, a limited amount of people meet that sort of freedom of time and financial burden. Also, explore the financial options if you choose to take a boot camp. I have seen some are accepted by the GI Bill as a higher education option. Some states and organizations will offer workforce and readiness grants to aid in some or all of the costs of the program.

I don't want to deride the boot camps because they can be good experience. With every choice that requires taking on significant financial burden, thoroughly examine everything they are saying. Most of the boot camps are offered by companies looking to still turn some kind of profit. If the admissions person you talk to makes any claims, ask them for the statistics and analysis that can back up that claim. An admission officer may try to tell you that "XYZ Academy can help you get a job, we have over a 90% placement rate with a first-year salary of over $60,000." When you actually sign the admissions paperwork, though, they will have a line that reads, "XYZ Academy does not guarantee you will find a job within any timeframe in the studied category or meeting any minimum salary requirements." The admissions contract you sign will indemnify them and most likely include a clause not allowing you to seek refunds, possibly even outlining an agreement by you to not speak badly of them either.

A coding boot camp could teach you extremely well. Or it could come down to a training exercise in how to Google and a structured set of projects you complete in teams while self-teaching a language via Google and tutorials. If the coding boot camp you look at boils down to that, then ask yourself if you're better off with just using this book and saving $11,990.

Open Source Projects

An open-source project is a piece of software built by a collective of people. Open source projects typically are released with licenses that allow free use in development and commercial practices. This doesn't mean they are bad products, entirely the opposite. A good open-source product with people that believe in the ideal of what they are building will make a fantastic piece of software. It also doesn't mean that everyone working on it were working for free. IBM, Adobe and many other large corporate enterprises have committed time and paid engineering resources to be contributors and stewards of various open-source projects. Also, just because the product is commercially available for free doesn't mean there is no monetization. Many companies exist to provide consultancy and support for open-source software systems.

The key point here is that open source projects need more people. You can find an open-source project written in any language. The Apache Software Foundation keeps a listing of all Apache-based projects, you can even sort through a listing based on language.

When you've decided on a project that interests you, you can browse the whole codebase before even making a commitment. That is another guiding principle of an open-source project. By having the whole source code open for anyone to view, it should reduce security issues as anyone can find them and suggest a fix. This benefits a new developer because now you can see how an entire Enterprise level application looks and is built.

When you find a project you want to work with, just look through their website. The project will generally have a page detailing how to become a contributor. A great first step would be to introduce yourself, tell them what you've been learning and you're looking to get some solid experience. See if you can work with them on bugs and very small features. This will allow you to have some points you can put on your resume, but also get you into the process of changing an existing codebase, doing code reviews (probably via a pull request), and working in a team.

This can also be a fantastic networking opportunity. The people you are working with could be working for any number of companies. They could help you find that first actual paying job by recognizing your ability and willingness to work and learn. So, while you won't be getting paid for the open-source contributions, it's still benefitting you in many ways.

Volunteering

In the same vein as an open-source project, you may already be involved or close to some organization in your community that could need you.

Many organizations, especially non-profits or lower budget ones, just don't have the funding to pay for much or any technical staffing. These groups are likely to be more than happy to take on people willing to help with building software for them for either low or no payment.

These organizations could be anything from the church or religious group you attend, to the school where your children are students, to a library, or even a homeless shelter. They all generally have a need for someone to help automate a database, make updates to a website, build email templates or mailing lists, etc. These are all valuable experiences to add to your resume. Again, it may not actually get you paid, but if you are looking at migrating into a coding career as a process that can take between 6 months to a year, then this can be a worthwhile way to do it.

Another big positive with volunteering is that you can keep the networking going here too. Anyone you work with in the process, be sure to keep emails, connect with on LinkedIn, etc. For projects completed with a group, even if they don't know someone looking to hire for your career goal, they can still write a letter of recommendation or provide endorsements on LinkedIn. Don't discount this. Having a resume loaded with projects is great, but having a pocket of people that will recommend you and be references is invaluable and necessary.

Friends and Family

I'm guessing if you are starting this journey to change careers, you've probably talked to some of your family and friends about it. They can be valuable resources as well. While you probably wouldn't want to have a resume point about building a personal website for your mother's recipe collection, you could reword it as, "Provided independent web design and implementation to organize and educate multicultural cuisine."

Ask around, and you may find that some of your friends have side things they do that could benefit from something you are looking to do. Perhaps they buy from local auctions to sell on eBay, and you can write something to help them automate postings. Maybe you even have a friend that is an amateur author or makes scented candles but has no online presence for sales/information.

These are, again, instances of experience that can easily go on resumes. The contacts can be used as references, though, anyone sharing the same last name may be a bit suspect. So, while you may get no payment, low payment, or even a barter exchange, the experience is the valuable point.

Freelancing

One option I've seen people take to both get experience and get at least some kind of a paycheck is freelancing. You can sign up on sites like upwork.com or freelancer.com, among others. When you sign up, they will have codes of conduct and guides on how it works. Usually, you apply for gigs that can be part-time, full-time, an exact number of hours, ongoing, etc.

With the jobs, they also offer skills assessments. The idea being, that if you want to take on some gigs in JavaScript or PHP, you can take an assessment for beginner, middle-levels, or expert in that language or topic. The assessment may even be required prior to applying or certain gigs.

Freelancing can be a great way to network and build experience while also getting paid, anywhere from $10/hour up. There are pitfalls to this approach though. The first thing is to beware of the post and poster for any red flags. Usually, the site like Upwork or Freelancer will have some way to guarantee you get paid for your work. Even with that guarantee, I'd be more hesitant to apply for a gig with a client that shows they've never paid anyone yet. If I've seen that they have a history of existing contracts, that makes me more confident that I would get paid.

Be very wary of flat-rate contracts. These can get more competitive than you may wish. For example, they may request someone to do a task and the payment is a flat rate of $50. If it's a task you know you can do in an hour, then a $50/hour gig seems great. If the requirements are something new to you, then it could become a twenty-hour task. Now you'll be getting the same $50, but it becomes a rate of only $2.50 per hour. That can be fine as a learning experience and something to get on your resume, but it doesn't lead to long term financial stability.

When you take on a project, stay as close to your commitments as possible. It will reflect poorly on you as a provider if you continually quote a task can be done in two days, but always go over your timeline. Being honest upfront about expectations will benefit both you and your client. This will be reflected in ratings/reviews left for you by those clients on the freelancing site and their connections/recommendations of you in the future.

If you make over a certain amount in a month, these sites are required by law to report your paid income to the Internal Revenue Service. They **do not** take out any payroll taxes when they pay you. **You** are solely responsible for determining your tax burden based on your income and paying that to local/state/federal governments. This can be done quarterly or annually. Do not forget this, you can be very sure the United States and IRS will not.

Freelancing may seem like a great way to make a ton of money as you get better at it. And, yes, it can. I've known people to go into freelancing beyond just the sites listed previously. They went into business for themselves and had many long term client relationships, able to charge well above $75/hour and stipulate overtime pay. Remember, this also means you don't get paid time off. Any time you take a vacation will cost you money. You are then responsible for finding health care coverage, which is not cheap. Also, see the previous paragraph regarding taxes. I can't stress enough, pay your taxes.

Tax software can do it if you don't want to deal with a Certified Public Accountant (CPA), but be sure to pay your taxes. You can write off a lot of expenses freelancing, like a home office (see IRS guidelines), computer equipment, mileage for client meetings, etc. Most commercial tax software will walk you through how to do this too.

One last thing to consider, if you go into freelancing for the long term, keep a rainy day fund. There will be economic downturns that cause your business and contracts to slow. If this is a route you want to take, keep enough reserves that you can survive work droughts.

CHAPTER 4

Looking For Work

"Anyone who is capable of getting themselves made President should on no account be allowed to do the job."

— *Douglas Adams,* **The Restaurant at the End of the Universe**

If you've made it to this point in the book, then either you've got some experience and are ready to find a job or you just kept on reading to be curious where I was going. Either way, congratulations! You're still intent on getting a job and haven't been deterred either by the education and experience or at least by the possibility of doing that.

I have had several roles over my 16 years of experience, technically more if you count the couple of dev related jobs in college. I've found some strategies for looking for a job to be more successful than others. I'll discuss those methods in this chapter. They can be as beneficial when looking for your eighth job as when looking for your first. Hell, they're probably generic enough you could use the same tactics searching for work in any professional field.

Location

I've mentioned it in an earlier chapter about doing job searching to help you determine what programming language(s) you should learn. With any luck, location is a decision that's easy for you. However, if you aren't tied down or are still young and adventurous, then changing locations can be a great thing to consider.

To be blunt, there are a lot more coding jobs available in bigger cities. The biggest market is San Francisco and Silicon Valley. However, there's a ton of developers in the San Francisco Bay Area too. Plus, there are more companies in Silicon Valley hiring remotely than ever.

In thinking of location, remember that a job is just that: a job. It earns you income to sustain your lifestyle. If you want to define yourself with your work, that's your business to do so. However, I'd advise against moving to a city just because of a job and a paycheck.

I could probably write a small handbook in just the decision factors for relocation and moving, but here are some top considerations.

Availability: Start surfing all the various job posting sites for an area you are thinking of living. Look at the volume of jobs in that market. A harder number to find will be how many other developers in that market are looking for the same job. Some of the job sites will show you a job, for example, an Entry Level/Junior Software Engineer role at Zillow. Some sites will also include how many other candidates have applied for that same job. Depending on the role and how well you align with it, the more candidates will dilute your chances of getting a job offer.

Salary/Cost of Living: These two factors go together and will be a make or break for the location. Larger markets with a higher cost of living will result in higher-paying jobs. The same job with the same benefits for the exact same corporation may pay $120k in San Francisco, $110k in Chicago, and $85k in Indianapolis. This is plausible with the expansion of some of the tech giants like Google, Amazon, Salesforce, etc. They have a high demand for developers and multiple headquarter and branch locations in many major cities.

Initially, that $120k in San Francisco would sound like the best deal. That comes out to an even $10k per month, right? Federal taxes will be the same across the board, but then you have state and local taxes to consider. At the time of this writing, California had a top tax rate of 12%, Illinois 6%, but Indiana 4%. Local taxes would likely be lower as well, and your sales taxes in the area would vary too. The general costs of food and entertainment differ, and the cost of a residence will be drastically different.

A reasonable example is the cost of renting an average one-bedroom apartment. In Chicago, that's $1650 per month, $3600 in San Francisco, and only $700 in Indianapolis. Also, the number of available living spaces may vary, you will probably find apartment hunting harder in San Francisco than other cities.

In real world and practice, you can find apartments for less in the Bay Area, and I do know people that don't pay more than $2000 per month. Just be aware the volume of housing may require you to make some compromises for living in a bigger metropolitan area.

The cost of living can be quantified though, and there are sites that offer detailed comparisons and basic indices. If you are having a difficult time with selecting a city or job market, comparing a selection of your top five markets will help narrow it down.

Entertainment/Community: Culturally, you may require or enjoy a certain market over another. I would say a city like Indianapolis offers a larger selection and a more hospitable attitude now than it did 30 years ago. However, so do New York and Los Angeles. If you're looking for a certain scene of immense culinary options, vibrant new music, and an extremely reliable and sprawling public transit system, then Indianapolis is not a good option. There aren't as many restaurant and entertainment venues, obviously, but we barely have a bus system that would be reliable enough to not own a car. If you live in Chicago, there are trains and buses, San Francisco has the BART, and New York has subways. Those are all reliable mass transit systems. A city like Indianapolis, though, had obvious suburban planning in mind so you have to drive everywhere.

Schools: An obvious issue if you have children or are looking forward to having children in the future. Making plans early on your location should consider that some public and private school options in larger metropolitan areas may not meet expectations. This isn't just an issue with New York City, either. The Indianapolis Public School system has had underperforming schools with just as bad problems too. However, some of the nearby suburbs can offer better options. This is an easy point to research though. Real Estate sites will show you local schools and their ratings/grades.

There is no silver bullet to making a location decision. It comes down to what you like and comfort. I live in a state like Indiana because there are enough metro areas I enjoy, but I also like a very low real estate cost with higher quality schools for my kids. Granted, my political leanings are more liberal, so living in a very conservative state can be challenging. But, I take that into weight together with what family I still have in the area and the spending power my income gives me for the region, and I come back to believing that staying where I am in Lebanon, IN is a better choice for me and my family than moving them to Seattle for a higher paycheck.

Worst case scenario, if you can find the right company, you could stay where you are and just work remotely. Picking up a remote job is becoming easier year by year. Entry-level is a bit more challenging to get a work from home kind of job, but still possible. I'll cover some more details about the differences around working from home in the next chapter.

LinkedIn and Job Sites

Beginning your job search for a coding role will most likely start at LinkedIn. LinkedIn is a social network for employment and business professionals. Like Facebook, you can connect with others, send messages, make posts, etc. Unlike Facebook, be more guarded about what you post. This is a business based network and any way you represent yourself will be considered by current or future employers. So it would be worth your restraint to avoid posting memes and dramatic political tirades. Anything you post should likely go through some spell and grammar checks too, as you are presenting yourself professionally and want to show you can communicate with sense.

What you should be doing on LinkedIn is finding

anyone you know or have worked with professionally, anyone you've dealt with for education, any professional contact at all and connect with them. Post all of your resume and keep it updated on your profile. This is not a time to be modest, either. You are trying to get a job, and you are your own best trumpeter. Any project you worked on, small or large, should be noted on your profile, even if it's an educational work. If you have deployed a site to some server that is accessible, even if it's a subdomain of a Heroku server, then link it back to your profile.

Once you have your resume and profile fully filled out, you can move onto a job hunt with LinkedIn. Changing some profile settings will allow tech recruiters to see you are looking for work and open to contact. Be aware though, recruiters cast a very wide net when fishing for candidates. They may contact you for a role you aren't interested in either due to the company, job description or location. Never feel pressured to apply for every opening.

If you opt to pay extra, you can also get LinkedIn Premium. Premium will give you extra features, like showing you a percentage match for your skill set and job openings, expected salary for positions, and a limited number of times you can message someone directly that has no connection with you on LinkedIn. The price of Premium may be worth it to you, and you may get a free month to try it out before having to pay.

Aside from LinkedIn, many other sites offer aid

in finding jobs or researching potential employers. Glassdoor.com allows you to not only search for job openings, but it provides a place for workers to leave anonymous reviews and ratings for companies. So, you can look at a company like Google and see how other employees rated them. You can also drill down to the job title you are looking to take at that company and see what the average ratings are of the company across that group, in case that department may have a better or worse opinion than others. One of Glassdoor's best features though, is the salary reports. You can see what others in that role have reported for annual salary to gauge what you can expect, along with how good the benefits may be.

There are many other sites for finding work, too many to really mention. Among them, some of the best sources will include Stack Overflow's jobs board, dice.com, and weworkremotely.com. The last site is a bit simpler, but deals entirely with positions for working remotely. It may be harder on that site to find entry-level roles too, but it could be worth coming back to for mid-level roles once you have a few years of experience.

Leveraging Contacts

In the previous section, I discussed how to use LinkedIn. Part of that discussion was you should connect with anyone you have worked with professionally. When you do, ask them if you can use them for references. When you apply for a professional job, you'll generally be expected to have at least three references. Having letters of reference or recommendations would be helpful as well. You can get these via LinkedIn with your contacts, but having physical copies would be advisable.

Aside from being references, your contacts and connections can be a great source of opportunities too. Not every company will list their job openings on LinkedIn, GlassDoor, or any major career site. In which case, just asking around with people you've worked with could be great for generating leads on a job. Sending a quick email or instant message just asking if they have or know of any openings could be the lead you can use to kickstart your career.

For example, some companies I've worked for may not have had openings. However, in my career and time I've spent on LinkedIn, I have connected with a number of tech recruiters. So, even if I don't have a role open in my company, I may have seen something from a recruiter or could put a friend in contact with some recruiters that could help a person find an entry-level role.

Keep up with anyone you've worked with while learning and getting your base experience. I would lay odds they have a similar network available to them and they could probably put you onto some leads, if not a job directly.

Social Media

A quick note about social media: clean it up. Employers won't be looking at your profile on Tinder, but anything you have tied to your name online may be found. I would advise you do a curation of your Twitter profile and change your privacy settings on Facebook to only Friends and not Public. A good general rule of thumb would be if you think saying the post out loud on the job would get you fired, then you should probably delete it—same thing for photos or videos showing drinking or drug use. You won't gain any employability points by showing you smoking up a massive joint to celebrate 4/20.

Interviews

Job interviews will be likely the most intimidating part of your process. Not just because you're meeting new people, but because you are trying to impress them enough to stand out among a field of other qualified candidates. The best advice I can give is to read. There are many sites and books that will talk specifically about coding interviews, and they will be very helpful.

Here's a general view of the process most companies use though. You apply for a role, and the hiring manager will collect the resumes. If they are interested in you, they'll contact you to set up a phone screen. A phone screen will usually be about a half-hour between you and either a recruiter or a hiring manager.

After a phone screening, the process can differ from company to company. Large scale firms like Google, Amazon, Salesforce, etc., may make the next step to be a coding test/tech interview. Sometimes this can be getting onto an online meeting with another engineer, or a timed challenge on a site like HackerRank or LeetCode.

Regardless of the extra step of a coding test, the last step will likely be a longer onsite interview. This could be a large group interview with many interviewers for one to two hours, or a series of shorter half to one-hour interviews with one or two people at a time. Some places will even want you to come do these interviews and have lunch with them. They're going to be looking for multiple things. The interviews will discuss your experiences, your aspirations, test you on basic computer science and computational skills on whiteboards, and get a feel for your personality and drive.

Don't Panic. These things will feel like a serious source of anxiety. For all the resumes and applications you send out, you may hear back from less than a quarter of them. Of those, you may go through the whole hiring process numerous times before you get a job offer. Don't Panic. These are, unfortunately, all natural and expected in this industry. If you don't get an offer, there is no harm in asking for feedback. Don't be surprised if they choose not to provide any though. Human Resources departments are more concerned about limiting their liabilities than helping an unhired candidate. The best thing you can do for yourself is keep a thick-skin, keep trying, and don't panic.

Always send a thank you note or email. Even if you don't get contacted again or don't get the job. It sends a message in the community that you are a courteous and professional person.

Accepting a Job Offer

One last thing to be prepared for will be a job offer. It may be the last thing you expect. It is something you should prepare for, though. If you don't, you may flounder around and undersell yourself. This is a case where you need to have done your research on places like GlassDoor and other career sites. Have an expected salary range you think you should be worth for an entry-level developer in your geographical area. Other factors will change what a company offers. Factors like the size of company, the kind of debt they currently hold and their economic viability, what kinds of other benefits they may offer, etc.

Be aware, no two job offers are equal. If you are confronted with multiple offers, then you need to be prepared to gauge which to accept on what is most important to you. This may mean you take a job with a firm that doesn't offer you the highest salary. Other benefits may outweigh some extra cash, like better insurance, higher performance-based bonuses, residual stock options, paid time off, etc.

When you get one you want to accept, the hiring

manager, recruiter or HR person will help you along the rest of the process. Usually, that starts with signing off on an offer letter. The offer should detail the job title and terms of employment, including your salary. Also, be aware if the salary is negotiated for an annual rate, you shouldn't be expecting over-time pay. You will be being paid for doing a job. This job can be most times a forty-hour work week, but sometimes, to do the job you'll be putting in some overtime. That's a trade off, you can expect bet-ter job security, benefits and opportunities, but you lose the random opportunity of time and a half pay rates for overtime. Consulting and freelancing can be an exception to this rule.

CHAPTER 5

So Long and Thanks for NOT Microwaving the Fish

"Ford carried on counting quietly. This is about the most aggressive thing you can do to a computer, the equivalent of going up to a human being and saying "Blood...blood...blood...blood..."

— *Douglas Adams, **The Hitchhiker's Guide to the Galaxy***

A lot of books focus on how to learn software development and get a job. One thing I've found lacking is their ability to prep a person for the soft skills and what to expect when they get into a job. That's what I want to discuss in this chapter. I want to show you what to expect and how to deal with some of the day-to-day parts of working in software development. This chapter may be of special use to the intrepid new developer that has never worked in an office setting before.

Honesty

My second full-time development role was with a consulting company. It was my first time with a consulting firm, but my manager gave me some very helpful advice. Always be completely honest. He was talking about dealing with our client, as I was to be working with the head of Customer Satisfaction for a large multinational corporation, but it is the best advice for anywhere. He told me this because he had seen other developers make a few mistakes in the past around trying to skimp timelines or suggest something without researching. When someone had done this, my manager had said our client could see right through it and would tear them down. The other downside was that now the client didn't trust that person anymore.

I don't mean you should embrace brutal honesty. You shouldn't go around the office and tell Dale in Accounting he really doesn't need a second donut, and likely didn't need the first, or any that he's eaten in the past seven years. But when someone asks you a question, don't try to pass some BS. It may work now and again, but I will guarantee you will be called out on it sometime.

For example, if someone asks me how long a project will take from start to finish, I give them a couple of estimates. I give them the average case, the best and worst-case scenarios. I also remind them they are estimates and they can change depending on the priorities of the company and possible unknown factors.

Especially starting, you will often be asked a question you don't know an answer. There is never a problem with admitting you don't know something, and no one will expect you to be omniscient. There are many ways to phrase the response too. "I'm not familiar with that, I can research it though and get back to you." "I haven't dealt with a task like that before, so I'm unable to gauge a definite timeframe." Those are just a couple of ways to admit you don't know something, but can work on figuring it out.

Cursing

A workplace for a developer is generally a professional environment. That doesn't mean you won't hear cursing and foul language. Depending on the office and your coworkers, they may have some minimal cursing or there may be an untethered carpet bombing of expletives to challenge careers in the Navy.

In my experience, I've seen many points on that sliding scale. I had one coworker that sat behind me in a developer's room. The room had desks to sit about eight of us. My coworker would usually listen to loud black metal on his headphones. We couldn't hear it, but it also kept him from hearing how loud he was himself. So, every time he hit a place where he forgot a semi-colon, something didn't compile right, or hit an error, the room would be serenaded by an artistically woven selection of the seven words you can't say on TV.

The best advice I can give you about this is to slip into it like a hot tub: slowly. Don't waltz in and drop f-bombs the first day. Listen to your coworkers and gradually adjust your tone as you feel comfortable. The primary caveat to this being don't use that same language with a client, customer or end-user. Watch your speech patterns around them and just make a practice of always being more guarded with what you say.

Office Politics

You will encounter office politics. You may not recognize it right away, but the longer you work in any office environment, you recognize the subtle and overt symptoms of office politics. You'll find some form of it in every office. Regardless of how much a company tries to minimize it, there will always be some people with hidden agendas. Maybe Dwight's angling to be Assistant Regional Manager seems harmless enough until he hounds your job performance to make himself look better.

At one office I worked in, there was a guy, we'll call him Bigfoot to save myself any legal issues as

Bigfoot can't sue me. I never worked with Bigfoot day-to-day, but he had a higher title in some client engagement role and was really looking to impress people. Bigfoot can't develop squatch though (sorry, had to make that pun somewhere). So, he needed to show a prototype of something to a client, and decided it needed to be done before the next day. So, just as I was wrapping up my day around 4:30 and sending my last emails, Bigfoot plopped himself in the opening of my cubicle.

I tried to politely tell Bigfoot I was done for the day and it could wait. Bigfoot tried to bribe me, a six-pack of beer if I'd be willing to work a little late and get that done for him. I figured it was an easy task anyway and relented, left about an hour later and it didn't cost me much. I didn't hear back from Bigfoot again, no beer either, which ticked me off. If you're going to offer something in exchange for using someone for your personal gain, at least pay the tab.

I randomly ran into the company president during a Habitat for Humanity build a month later. I asked about Bigfoot's presentation and recounted my tale. The president was shocked. The next day, I had a six-pack of my favorite Bock on my desk, and I never had to deal with Bigfoot again.

There is a lesson from that story on positive office politics too. As you get into a job, you will start to pick up on the power structures, the organizational charts, the idea of who really has the ability to affect change. I was affected by the negative political movements of Bigfoot, so I took advantage of being in proximity to a person that can affect more change. By giving a subtle nudge, I got Bigfoot to deliver on his promise while delivering a message of my own indirectly.

I don't encourage anyone to play negative office politics. It's as slimy on the small scale as it is at a macro level. However, I would advise you to read *The Art of War* by Sun Tzu. It is a tactics guide, very small, written by the ancient Chinese military strategist Sun Tzu around the 5th century BC. You can find some translations that will give explanations and examples in a corporate setting. If you read that and *The Prince* by Machiavelli, you stand a good chance of recognizing any attempts to draw you into office politics and how to shut them down. *Hamlet* and *Julius Caesar* by Shakespeare wouldn't be bad additions either.

Office Romance

Don't. No. Yes, I get you might be attracted to someone, but stop. This is your work environment, not a bar. If you need intimacy, then join a dating site or hookup app like Tinder. While it's perfectly fine to be friendly and have dinner or drinks with your coworkers in a social setting, leave it at that.

If you find yourself really wanting to start a relationship with a coworker, put in some due diligence. Check your company's employee handbook on intraoffice relationships. Some firms will have a policy like, "you're allowed to ask once, if they say 'no', don't press it. If you ask again, you're out."

Some may say that sounds harsh for some innocent flirting, but put yourself in the other's shoes. The other person may orient themselves sexually different from you. It wouldn't be a healthy work environment if you faced coming into work every day to face pick up lines and someone that just can't understand being told no. That could be construed as hostile.

Overall, it's just easier on everyone to avoid it. You can find much easier ways to hook up anymore without doing it at the office. You may think you'll be finding a soulmate, but what you might actually find is a lot of awkwardness and drama that didn't need to exist in the first place.

Walking Away/Balance

One thing that should be important to you coming into any job is having a good work/life balance. You'll hear that term a lot, work/life balance. But what is it? It's the ability to find a lack of opposition between your personal and professional life.

For example, if you are working a lot of overtime, that will affect your personal life. If you have a family, they will hate you and your job for never spending time with them. Even if you have no family though, constant work will make you burnt out and you will hate your job.

On the other side, your employer wants to help

you manage this too. If you're constantly away from work, then your employer won't be happy with you. However, employers know that if they burn you out, then you'll find another job and leave them. An employer usually has a vested interest in keeping you, as finding someone to replace you and training that person will cost them valuable time and money.

Also, regarding balance, the first few years as a white-collar software engineer can feel a bit blurry. Work doesn't mean just the coding aspects, and a social gathering isn't always a part of your personal life. Meeting up for a company dinner with a date and having drinks may sound like a social event and a part of personal life, but these are still your co-workers. You still would end up being more guarded and keeping a different mask with them then you might at home, so that's still a part of your work life. Conversely, you may really enjoy coding certain things and do some side things for yourself. So, if you are coding after hours, on your own equipment, for a goal only worthy to yourself, then it's no longer a part of work.

Aside from a general work/life balance, be aware that any problem in software development can easily become a brick wall. Banging your head against that wall will not break it down or solve the problem. Something I learned early in my career is that there's value in walking away from something for a while. Give yourself short breaks when you feel stuck and do something like take a walk or a run, grab something to eat, read a book, try out a tutorial in something. Basically, just get away from that problem for a while. Leaving it alone for 20-30 minutes or overnight could prove to help you see something you missed or a way to solve your problem.

Finally, with work hours, you should really have a discussion with your manager on how to approach them. Changing careers from an hourly job or some other industries into software can be much less restrictive. You may be used to a job that has set hours, clock in at 9 am, clock out at 5 pm and done. If you are a salary worker, your manager may not care for you to be stuck in front of your screen for the whole forty hours. A lot of companies are fine with knocking off early or keeping closer to 35-37 hour weeks since they'll ask you to deal with the overtime now and then. Work hours can also vary, some people like to get on early around 5 am and be done at 2 pm, others may like a 10 am to 6 pm routine. Most companies are adaptable enough around these schedules for it to not be an issue.

Don't be a D!ck

This should be self-explanatory. It could go along with the office politics section, but sometimes people are just really nasty to one another. It's a pretty simple principle, like the golden rule, etc.: Treat others how you want to be treated. That doesn't mean yelling in meetings to get your way.

That doesn't mean treating everyone like your time is more valuable. That doesn't mean saying things or making jokes that are sexist or racist. Try just thinking before you speak, if it's not something you would appreciate being said to you or at least a constructive criticism, then don't say it.

Never Stop Learning

You did a ton of learning to get a job in development in the first place. You learned one or more new programming languages, learned a lot about process and development life cycles. You probably feel like you've crammed a lot of new information in your head. Don't stop.

As a new software developer, coder, engineer, whatever title you place on yourself, you are now facing a career where you cannot stop learning. There will always be new languages, techniques, etc., to expand your knowledge base. The programmers I've seen that stop learning either do one of two things. They either go into management where they don't need to code as much anymore or they stagnate. By stagnate, I mean they may continue with the level where they are at, but they'll likely never see any more promotions, and at some point, they'll see raises decrease too.

Lucky for you, there are a lot of resources for learning. You've already been using a lot of them if you followed this guide and didn't skip ahead for spoilers. Aside from the freebies though, you've got options. LinkedIn has a learning segment for training and tutorials, it was formerly lynda.com but was acquired in 2015. There are other sites for paid learning. Also, you can try coding challenges at places like HackerRank or LeetCode.

There are also numerous conferences across the world for any language or job-specific function. If you aspire to other higher education, you could also look into college courses, either at a local college or online. These options may change what you are looking for in a company too. A lot of companies will have a declared amount they are willing or able to spend towards continuing education for employees every year. This could be limited to subscriptions for an account with O'Reilly Media for their extensive programming manuals, or as broad as $3-10k per year for classes and conferences. Ask about this in interviews, but also ask if there are any stipulations. Some companies will offer the continuing education options, but put conditions on them such as that you must remain in their employ for a length of time or you'll agree to repay a percentage back to the company.

Expenses

At some point in your professional career, you will be taking business trips. These can be related to working with clients or conferences for education. Your company should be paying for your expenses on these trips since it is all work-related. They will have policies in their manual on how to handle it.

Depending on the company, they will either reimburse you afterward or issue you a company credit card. There are two important things to remember. One, keep every receipt you intend to expense, regardless if you use a company card. Accountants are notorious for needing a paper trail on literally everything. Two, check your company's manual on expenses or per diem. Most will have an outline of what you are allowed, like they won't pay for inflight WiFi or not over $15 at any given meal.

If you are traveling with someone who has more seniority, defer to their judgment. In cases where I've been traveling with someone with more seniority, I've even just deferred to letting them pay with their company card. That may sound like less freedom, but I still ate and they had to deal with the expense reports.

From another aspect, you shouldn't short change yourself when spending company money either. As long as you are working towards the ideal of what the company expects, then it's normally fine. I'll give a couple of examples. Some firms I've worked with have had expense policies with meals that also allow reasonable alcohol consumption. So, it is not outside the bounds of reason for a meal while on a company trip could be sushi and a beer. Just because the per diem policy lists "under $20 per meal average", doesn't mean your company expects you to order from a dollar menu for meals. Now, if I was on a business trip, but met up with three friends from high school and used my company card to get dinner and drinks for all of us, then I'd be violating the company's trust.

Another Example of an expense situation would be my friend. He and I worked for the same company at the time, and we both worked remotely. He used his company card to expense an office chair. It was a fairly nice chair. When his manager got the expense report though, she wasn't happy about it. He countered back, "if I were working in HQ, would you provide me a chair?" She conceded the point and approved it, but warned him about getting prior approval in the future. But he did have a point, the company had a policy to cover that and he exercised it.

Lesson here being, the policies and budgets exist for a reason. Utilize them as needed. Always do your best to use them wisely, but use them.

Working From Home

I wrote this book mostly while the United States and most of the world was shut down for the Covid-19 pandemic. Offices were closed and most tech companies moved everyone to work from home where possible. It wasn't the first time I've worked from home, not even the first time doing it full time. Working remotely can be one of the absolute best perks of taking a career in software development. Technology has come so far in recent decades I can work with a team not only remote, but multinational. It cuts the commute time considerably, I don't have to spend 20-30 minutes driving to an office every day. Just shower and hop online.

It can be quite an adjustment for coders that have never done it full time. During the first weeks of the Covid-19 pandemic, workers had varying degrees of coping with the temporary and ongoing changes. Some, like myself, were used to it and just adjusted to other aspects, such as suddenly having kids learning at home too. Others had a harder time adjusting, some even seeming to mourn the loss of an office suddenly unavailable to them.

There are some good lessons to take in to help adjust from working in an office to working from home. Try to maintain a routine. By keeping a schedule day to day, like you would with an office, it helps keep your brain in mode for getting your work done. Take breaks though, sitting in front of a laptop all day will get monotonous and burn you out. It's worthwhile to even take a couple of breaks a bit longer for walking the dog or going for a jog or bike ride.

Create a setup separate from your living space if possible. This may not be an easy task in smaller apartments. If you can manage it, set aside either a small room or a corner that has just a desk and can be your home office. Try to set it up as close to an office as you'd expect, ergonomic chair and desk help, but also making sure your internet access reaches the area, lighting is good and you can exercise some privacy. Don't work from bed or a couch.

It may seem good every now and then, but it will be pure hell on your back after a while.

There are many other lessons to working from home, and entire blogs and websites designed to help. If you'll be taking on a job during a time when offices are still shuddered or looking into a completely remote position, take time to research these sites more.

Leaving a Job

At some point in your career you will decide to change jobs. The likelihood of staying at one company for an entire career in any technical role is very low. Depending on the company, the average tenure will be between 1.5 to 3 years. The larger companies get a longer tenure from workers, but the turnover is still there. People leave jobs for many reasons, they decide that they need a change of pace, wages aren't good enough, benefits decrease, or they just tire of some of their coworkers.

Regardless the reason you want to leave your job, think it out thoroughly before making a change. Unless you have a savings of a half year worth of salary, don't just yell, "I quit!" It may not be an advantageous time to do so. The most beneficial thing would be to ask yourself if you are happy with everything in your job every six months. If you generally are or don't believe your situation would improve elsewhere, then stay another six months.

If your answer is that you aren't happy, though,

then it's time to start up the hunt. Updating resume, LinkedIn, getting recommendations, etc. Unless you are extremely comfortable with the company you are with, do not ask your present employer to be a reference. Do not announce to your current employer that you are looking at changing jobs. It can cause bad reactions. They may try to fix things for you, which is great. Some issues aren't resolvable though, or outside of their control. In which case, they may fire you instead of letting you continue to work in their code base. So, discretion is usually the best route.

Take vacation time or schedule interviews outside of your normal working hours. Be aware of your social media presence. While you can hide a lot of what you're doing on LinkedIn, nothing is stopping an employer from seeing your Twitter or Facebook accounts where you blatantly post how much you hate your job and are now looking for a new one. Again, discretion is key.

Before you start interviews, be prepared to answer the same question everyone will ask you, "Why are you leaving your current role?" When you get new job offers, be careful to consider everything from benefits and salary, to location and title. Sometimes you can advance your salary and receive better healthcare or time off by simply making a lateral move to do the same exact job for some other company.

When you do accept da new job, make some decisions about how you will leave your current one. Conventional wisdom is to provide a letter of resignation and two weeks' notice. Recently, I had read some people saying this is unnecessary. They argued that you are effectively firing your current employer, and since you aren't compelled by contracts to leave a two weeks notice, you can just quit and leave the same day. I would be careful of taking this route. Measure to yourself if you want to burn the bridges or leave them standing. If you give two weeks and are as cordial as you can stand for that time, then while your coworkers will still be sad to lose you, they can still be your friends and contacts in your professional network. Walking away suddenly could burn a bridge that you must cross again someday in the future.

SUGGESTED READING

Here are some great books I'd suggest to read along your journey. They aren't language specific, so they should all be helpful for most journeys into a coding career.

Martin, Robert C. (2008) *Clean Code: A Handbook of Agile Software Craftsmanship.* Prentice Hall.

Hunt, Andrew; Thomas, David. (2019) *The Pragmatic Programmer: From Journeyman to Master, 20th Annivesary Edition.* Addison-Wesley Professional.

McDowell, Gayle Laakmann. (2015) *Cracking the Coding Interview: 189 Programming Questions and Solutions.* CareerCup.

Subramaniam, Venkat; Hunt, Andy. (2006) *Practices of an Agile Developer: Working in the Real World.* Pragmatic Bookshelf.

Tzu, Sun. *The Art of War.*

Machiavelli, Nicollo. (2019) *The Prince.* SDE Classics.

Greene, Robert. (2000) *The 48 Laws of Power.* Penguin Books.

Martinez, Antonio Garcia. (2016) *Chaos Monkeys.* HarperCollins

AFTERWORD

Thanks for reading the Hitchhiker's Guide to Coding. I hope it has helped and encouraged you to start or continue your journey to a career in software development. I really do believe this book will benefit people and that it is possible to start and build an extremely rewarding career in software development and engineering without a degree in computer science.

Please remember to take a moment and leave a rating and review for this book. You can easily do so with a few words at http://amazon.com/review/create-review?&asin=B088182GK6

BOOKS BY THIS AUTHOR

Over A God's Dead Body

Three gods walk onto a college campus looking for a dead body. A bad joke, a bad day, or both? Esmy Hansen is about to find out.

Esmy is stuck in a rut and frustrated by a lack of pockets on women's pants. Meeting Loki ignites her life like a powder-keg. This simple, seemingly innocuous encounter leads her and Jake to discover the college campus's mysterious depths, involving sasquatches, vampires, and much more. In a crudely comedic high-stakes game of maneuvering, Loki's freedom and Esmy's survival come down to a fight over a God's dead body.

Over a God's Dead Body is the first book in a humorous supernatural series! If you like insane action, hilarious dialogue, and gods behaving badly, then you'll love the first installment in Joel Spriggs's magical comedy.

Buy Over a God's Dead Body to start the madcap misadventure today!

Another Dead Intern

There is nothing normal about an internship with Hemlock Connal, Preternatural Investigator!

Hemlock can't keep interns alive. Morgan Burns is trying to break that trend, but finds survival to be an uphill battle. Faced with mobsters, drug rings, covens, and even fantastical beasts, will Morgan find a paycheck... or a grave?

Another Dead Intern is the first book in a humorous supernatural mystery series! If you like edge-of-your-seat action, witty dialogue, and paranormal investigations, then you'll love the first installment in Joel Spriggs's hilarious magical thrill ride.

Buy Another Dead Intern to start the madcap fantastical adventure today!

Little Drummer Boy

A darkly humorous paranormal Christmas short!

Boston's strangest private investigator, Hemlock Connal, is back! Along with her longest surviving intern, Morgan Burns. When a demonic drummer boy

walks down their road leading a small team of zombies, the detective duo take a much needed break from a boring financial case.

As they follow the horned drummer from Boston to the middle of nowhere, they find the zombie squad has more secrets than just marching through the night. Hemlock and Morgan get led through a dark journey of black market organ theft, drug sorting undead, all leading up to meeting the big man himself.

Confronted with the ultimate arbiter of the holiday season, will Hemlock and Morgan survive the test of naughty or nice? Find out, in Little Drummer Boy!

The Bear Was Not There

"I looked over by my oscilloscopes," said my dad. "Near the Tesla coils, past the arc welder, and even in the corner with the Theremin. But the bear was not there. Then something really strange happened."

What began as a routine task of finding a treasured stuffed koala for his daughter, quickly turned into an adventure for one father. Along with a talking pet cat, he must follow the koala's trail to encounter werewolves, pixies, aliens, and more to achieve his original goal: getting his children to sleep.

If you like wild adventure, poorly drawn post-it notes, sci-fi, and fantasy all blended together, then you'll love this fantastical journey.

Buy The Bear Was Not There to start the madcap wondrous adventure today!

ABOUT THE AUTHOR

Joel Spriggs is a Software Engineer, Consultant and Author. Joel has been building a career in Software Engineering for over sixteen years. He holds a Bachelor's of the Fine Arts from Franklin College of Indiana in Computer Science and Broadcast Journalism. Aside from this book, Joel also writes fiction. You can find how to get any of his books and novels at his website, joelspriggs.com.